TO EMPOWER PEOPLE

The Role of Mediating Structures in Public Policy

Peter L. Berger
Richard John Neuhaus

American Enterprise Institute for Public Policy Research
Washington, D.C.

Peter L. Berger is professor of sociology at Rutgers University. Richard John Neuhaus is senior editor of *Worldview* magazine.

ISBN O-8447-3236-2

Library of Congress Catalog Card No. 76-58262

(Political and Social Processes 1) (AEI Studies 139)

Third printing, August 1979
Second printing, October 1977

Printed in the United States of America

CONTENTS

PREFACE

In 1975 the authors initiated a research project whose purpose was to explore the role of mediating structures in public policy. This essay introduces the basic idea of the project, suggests some possible policy implications, and indicates the areas and directions of future research effort. Since the project itself will continue through 1979 and since it is intended that it will result in several volumes of specific policy recommendations by different participants, the policy recommendations in this essay should be viewed only as suggestive of the directions agreed upon by the authors, who are the co-directors of the project. This is an American Enterprise Institute project, partially funded by the National Endowment for the Humanities.

The research being undertaken is clustered under five broad policy areas. Chairing the five panels are: health care—Ruth Aikens (National Council of Negro Women); housing and zoning—John Egan (University of Notre Dame); welfare and social services—Nathan Glazer (Harvard University); education and child care—David Seeley (Public Education Association); criminal justice—Robert Woodson (National Urban League). Theodore Michael Kerrine is the executive director of the project, which is based in New York City.

TO EMPOWER PEOPLE

I. MEDIATING STRUCTURES AND THE DILEMMAS OF THE WELFARE STATE

Two seemingly contradictory tendencies are evident in current thinking about public policy in America. First, there is a continuing desire
for the services provided by the modern welfare state. Partisan
rhetoric aside, few people seriously envisage dismantling the welfare
state. The serious debate is over how and to what extent it should
be expanded. The second tendency is one of strong animus against
government, bureaucracy, and bigness as such. This animus is directed
not only toward Washington but toward government at all levels.
Although this essay is addressed to the American situation, it should
be noted that a similar ambiguity about the modern welfare state
exists in other democratic societies, notably in Western Europe.

Perhaps this is just another case of people wanting to eat their
cake and have it too. It would hardly be the first time in history that
the people wanted benefits without paying the requisite costs. Nor
are politicians above exploiting ambiguities by promising increased
services while reducing expenditures. The extravagant rhetoric of the
modern state and the surrealistic vastness of its taxation system encourage magical expectations that make contradictory measures seem
possible. As long as some of the people can be fooled some of the
time, some politicians will continue to ride into office on such magic.

But this is not the whole story. The contradiction between wanting more government services and less government may be only
apparent. More precisely, we suggest that the modern welfare state
is here to stay, indeed that it ought to expand the benefits it provides—
but that *alternative mechanisms are possible to provide welfare-state
services.*

1

The current anti-government, anti-bigness mood is not irrational. Complaints about impersonality, unresponsiveness, and excessive interference, as well as the perception of rising costs and deteriorating service—these are based upon empirical and widespread experience. The crisis of New York City, which is rightly seen as more than a fiscal crisis, signals a national state of unease with the policies followed in recent decades. At the same time there is widespread public support for publicly addressing major problems of our society in relieving poverty, in education, health care, and housing, and in a host of other human needs. What first appears as contradiction, then, is the sum of equally justified aspirations. The public policy goal is to address human needs without exacerbating the reasons for animus against the welfare state.

Of course there are no panaceas. The alternatives proposed here, we believe, can solve *some* problems. Taken seriously, they could become the basis of far-reaching innovations in public policy, perhaps of a new paradigm for at least sectors of the modern welfare state.

The basic concept is that of what we are calling mediating structures. The concept in various forms has been around for a long time. What is new is the systematic effort to translate it into specific public policies. For purposes of this study, mediating structures are defined as *those institutions standing between the individual in his private life and the large institutions of public life.*

Modernization brings about an historically unprecedented dichotomy between public and private life. The most important large institution in the ordering of modern society is the modern state itself. In addition, there are the large economic conglomerates of capitalist enterprise, big labor, and the growing bureaucracies that administer wide sectors of the society, such as in education and the organized professions. All these institutions we call the *megastructures*.

Then there is that modern phenomenon called private life. It is a curious kind of preserve left over by the large institutions and in which individuals carry on a bewildering variety of activities with only fragile institutional support.

For the individual in modern society, life is an ongoing migration between these two spheres, public and private. The megastructures are typically alienating, that is, they are not helpful in providing meaning and identity for individual existence. Meaning, fulfillment, and personal identity are to be realized in the private sphere. While the two spheres interact in many ways, in private life the individual is left very much to his own devices, and thus is uncertain and anxious. Where modern society is "hard," as in the megastructures,

2

it is personally unsatisfactory; where it is "soft," as in private life, it cannot be relied upon. Compare, for example, the social realities of employment with those of marriage.

The dichotomy poses a double crisis. It is a crisis for the individual who must carry on a balancing act between the demands of the two spheres. It is a political crisis because the megastructures (notably the state) come to be devoid of personal meaning and are therefore viewed as unreal or even malignant. Not everyone experiences this crisis in the same way. Many who handle it more successfully than most have access to institutions that *mediate* between the two spheres. Such institutions have a private face, giving private life a measure of stability, and they have a public face, transferring meaning and value to the megastructures. Thus, mediating structures alleviate each facet of the double crisis of modern society. Their strategic position derives from their reducing both the anomic precariousness of individual existence in isolation from society and the threat of alienation to the public order.

Our focus is on four such mediating structures—neighborhood, family, church, and voluntary association. This is by no means an exhaustive list, but these institutions were selected for two reasons: first, they figure prominently in the lives of most Americans and, second, they are most relevant to the problems of the welfare state with which we are concerned. The proposal is that, if these institutions could be more imaginatively recognized in public policy, individuals would be more "at home" in society, and the political order would be more "meaningful."

Without institutionally reliable processes of mediation, the political order becomes detached from the values and realities of individual life. Deprived of its moral foundation, the political order is "delegitimated." When that happens, the political order must be secured by coercion rather than by consent. And when that happens, democracy disappears.

The attractiveness of totalitarianism—whether instituted under left-wing or right-wing banners—is that it overcomes the dichotomy of private and public existence by imposing on life one comprehensive order of meaning. Although established totalitarian systems can be bitterly disappointing to their architects as well as their subjects, they are, on the historical record, nearly impossible to dismantle. The system continues quite effectively, even if viewed with cynicism by most of the population—including those who are in charge.

Democracy is "handicapped" by being more vulnerable to the erosion of meaning in its institutions. Cynicism threatens it; wholesale cynicism can destroy it. That is why mediation is so crucial to democracy. Such mediation cannot be sporadic and occasional; it must be institutionalized in *structures*. The structures we have chosen to study have demonstrated a great capacity for adapting and innovating under changing conditions. Most important, they exist where people are, and that is where sound public policy should always begin.

This understanding of mediating structures is sympathetic to Edmund Burke's well-known claim: "To be attached to the subdivision, to love the little platoon we belong to in society, is the first principle (the germ as it were) of public affections." And it is sympathetic to Alexis de Tocqueville's conclusion drawn from his observation of Americans: "In democratic countries the science of association is the mother of science; the progress of all the rest depends upon the progress it has made." Marx too was concerned about the destruction of community, and the glimpse he gives us of post-revolutionary society is strongly reminiscent of Burke's "little platoons." The emphasis is even sharper in the anarcho-syndicalist tradition of social thought.

In his classic study of suicide, Emile Durkheim describes the "tempest" of modernization sweeping away the "little aggregations" in which people formerly found community, leaving only the state on the one hand and a mass of individuals, "like so many liquid molecules," on the other. Although using different terminologies, others in the sociological tradition—Ferdinand Toennies, Max Weber, Georg Simmel, Charles Cooley, Thorstein Veblen—have analyzed aspects of the same dilemma. Today Robert Nisbet has most persuasively argued that the loss of community threatens the future of American democracy.

Also, on the practical political level, it might seem that mediating structures have universal endorsement. There is, for example, little political mileage in being anti-family or anti-church. But the reality is not so simple. Liberalism—which constitutes the broad center of American politics, whether or not it calls itself by that name—has tended to be blind to the political (as distinct from private) functions of mediating structures. The main feature of liberalism, as we intend the term, is a commitment to government action toward greater social justice within the existing system. (To revolutionaries, of course, this is "mere reformism," but the revolutionary option has not been especially relevant, to date, in the American context.)

Liberalism's blindness to mediating structures can be traced to its Enlightenment roots. Enlightenment thought is abstract, universalistic, addicted to what Burke called "geometry" in social policy.

4

The concrete particularities of mediating structures find an inhospitable soil in the liberal garden. There the great concern is for the individual ("the rights of man") and for a just public order, but anything "in between" is viewed as irrelevant, or even an obstacle, to the rational ordering of society. What lies in between is dismissed, to the extent it can be, as superstition, bigotry, or (more recently) cultural lag.

American liberalism has been vigorous in the defense of the private rights of individuals, and has tended to dismiss the argument that private behavior can have public consequences. Private rights are frequently defended *against* mediating structures—children's rights against the family, the rights of sexual deviants against neighborhood or small-town sentiment, and so forth. Similarly, American liberals are virtually faultless in their commitment to the religious liberty of individuals. But the liberty to be defended is always that of privatized religion. Supported by a very narrow understanding of the separation of church and state, liberals are typically hostile to the claim that institutional religion might have public rights and public functions. As a consequence of this "geometrical" outlook, liberalism has a hard time coming to terms with the alienating effects of the abstract structures it has multiplied since the New Deal. This may be the Achilles heel of the liberal state today.

The left, understood as some version of the socialist vision, has been less blind to the problem of mediation. Indeed the term alienation derives from Marxism. The weakness of the left, however, is its exclusive or nearly exclusive focus on the capitalist economy as the source of this evil, when in fact the alienations of the socialist states, insofar as there are socialist states, are much more severe than those of the capitalist states. While some theorists of the New Left have addressed this problem by using elements from the anarcho-syndicalist tradition, most socialists see mediating structures as something that may be relevant to a post-revolutionary future, but that in the present only distracts attention from the struggle toward building socialism. Thus the left is not very helpful in the search for practical solutions to our problem.

On the right of the political broad center, we also find little that is helpful. To be sure, classical European conservatism had high regard for mediating structures, but, from the eighteenth century on, this tradition has been marred by a romantic urge to revoke modernity—a prospect that is, we think, neither likely nor desirable. On the other hand, what is now called conservatism in America is in fact old-style liberalism. It is the laissez-faire ideology of the period before the New Deal, which is roughly the time when liberalism shifted its faith from the market to government. *Both* the old faith in the market *and* the new faith in government share the abstract thought patterns of the Enlightenment. In addition, today's conservatism typically exhibits the weakness of the left in reverse: it is highly sensitive to the alienations of big government, but blind to the analogous effects of big business. Such one-sidedness, whether left or right, is not helpful.

As is now being widely recognized, we need new approaches free of the ideological baggage of the past. The mediating structures paradigm cuts across current ideological and political divides. This proposal has met with gratifying interest from most with whom we have shared it, and while it has been condemned as right-wing by some and as left-wing by others, this is in fact encouraging. Although the paradigm may play havoc with the conventional political labels, it is hoped that, after the initial confusion of what some social scientists call "cognitive shock," each implication of the proposal will be   own merits.

                          t of this essay—and the focus of the research project   introduce—can be subsumed under three proposi-   proposition is analytical: *Mediating structures are   tal democratic society.* The other two are broad   ommendations: *Public policy should protect and   structures,* and *Wherever possible, public policy   'iating structures for the realization of social pur-   h project will determine, it is hoped, whether these   up under rigorous examination and, if so, how   ted into specific recommendations.

The analytical proposition assumes that mediating structures are the value-generating and value-maintaining agencies in society. Without them, values become another function of the megastructures, notably of the state, and this is a hallmark of totalitarianism. In the totalitarian case, the individual becomes the object rather than the subject of the value-propagating processes of society.

The two programmatic propositions are, respectively, minimalist and maximalist. Minimally, public policy should cease and desist from damaging mediating structures. Much of the damage has been unintentional in the past. We should be more cautious than we have been. As we have learned to ask about the effects of government action upon racial minorities or upon the environment, so we should learn to ask about the effects of public policies on mediating structures.

6

The maximalist proposition ("utilize mediating structures") is much the riskier. We emphasize, "wherever possible." The mediating structures paradigm is not applicable to all areas of policy. Also, there is the real danger that such structures might be "co-opted" by the government in a too eager embrace that would destroy the very distinctiveness of their function. The prospect of government control of the family, for example, is clearly the exact opposite of our intention. The goal in utilizing mediating structures is to expand government services without producing government oppressiveness. Indeed it might be argued that the achievement of that goal is one of the acid tests of democracy.

It should be noted that these propositions differ from superficially similar proposals aimed at decentralizing governmental functions. Decentralization is limited to what can be done *within* governmental structures; we are concerned with the structures that stand *between* government and the individual. Nor, again, are we calling for a devolution of governmental responsibilities that would be tantamount to dismantling the welfare state. We aim rather at rethinking the institutional means by which government exercises its responsibilities. The idea is not to revoke the New Deal but to pursue its vision in ways more compatible with democratic governance.

Finally, there is a growing ideology based upon the proposition that "small is beautiful." We are sympathetic to that sentiment in some respects, but we do not share its programmati   the basic features of modern society. Our point is megastructures but to find better ways in which th the "little platoons" in our common life.

The theme is *empowerment*. One of the most de of modernization is a feeling of powerlessness in th tions controlled by those whom we do not know a we often do not share. Lest there be any doubt, c human beings, whoever they are, understand their (than anyone else—in, say, 99 percent of all cases. structures under discussion here are the principal e real values and the real needs of people in our society,   the most part, the people-sized institutions. Public policy should recognize, respect, and, where possible, empower these institutions.

A word about the poor is in order. Upper-income people already have ways to resist the encroachment of megastructures. It is not their children who are at the mercy of alleged child experts, not their health which is endangered by miscellaneous vested interests, not their neighborhoods which are made the playthings of utopian

7

income people may allow themselves to be victimized
s, but they do have ways to resist if they choose to
le have this power to a much lesser degree. The
ating structures aims at empowering poor people to
the more affluent can already do, aims at spreading
l a bit more—and to do so where it matters, in
ver their own lives. Some may call this populism.
been marred by utopianism and by the politics of
hoose to describe it as the empowerment of people.

II. NEIGHBORHOOD

"The most sensible way to locate the neighborhood," writes Milton
Kotler in *Neighborhood Government* (Bobbs-Merrill, 1969) "is to ask
people where it is, for people spend much time fixing its boundaries.
Gangs mark its turf. Old people watch for its new faces. Children
figure out safe routes between home and school. People walk their
dogs through their neighborhood, but rarely beyond it."

At first blush, it seems the defense of neighborhood is a mother-
hood issue. The neighborhood is the place of relatively intact and
secure existence, protecting us against the disjointed and threatening
big world "out there." Around the idea of neighborhood gravitate
warm feelings of nostalgia and the hope for community. It may not
be the place where we are entirely at home, but it is the place where
we are least homeless.

While no doubt influenced by such sentiments, the new interest
in neighborhoods today goes far beyond sentimentality. The neighborhood should be seen as a key mediating structure in the reordering
of our national life. As is evident in fears and confusions surrounding
such phrases as ethnic purity or neighborhood integrity, the focus
on neighborhood touches some of the most urgent and sensitive issues
of social policy. Indeed, many charge that the "rediscovery" of the
neighborhood is but another, and thinly veiled, manifestation of
racism.

Against that charge we contend—together with many others,
both black and white, who have a strong record of commitment to
racial justice—that strong neighborhoods can be a potent instrument
in achieving greater justice for all Americans. It is not true, for
example, that all-black neighborhoods are by definition weak neighborhoods. As we shall see, to argue the contrary is to relegate black
America to perpetual frustration or to propose a most improbable

program of social revolution. To put it simply, real community development must begin where people are. If our hopes for development assume an idealized society cleansed of ethnic pride and its accompanying bigotries, they are doomed to failure.

While social policy that can be morally approved must be attuned to the needs of the poor—and in America that means very particularly the black poor—the nonpoor also live in and cherish the values of neighborhood. The neighborhood in question may be as part-time and tenuous as the many bedroom communities surrounding our major cities; it may be the ethnic and economic crazy-quilt of New York's East Village; it may be the tranquil homogeneity of the east side of Cisco, Texas. Again, a neighborhood is what the people who live there say is a neighborhood.

For public policy purposes, there is no useful definition of what makes a good neighborhood, though we can agree on what constitutes a bad neighborhood. Few people would choose to live where crime is rampant, housing deteriorated, and garbage uncollected. To describe these phenomena as bad is not an instance of imposing middle-class, bourgeois values upon the poor. No one, least of all the poor, is opposed to such "middle class" values as safety, sanitation, and the freedom of choice that comes with affluence. With respect to so-called bad neighborhoods, we have essentially three public policy choices: we can ignore them, we can attempt to dismantle them and spread their problems around more equitably, or we can try to transform the bad into the better on the way to becoming good. The first option, although common, should be intolerable. The second is massively threatening to the nonpoor, and therefore not feasible short of revolution. The third holds most promise for a public policy that can gain the support of the American people. And, if we care more about consequence than about confrontation, the third is also the most radical in long-range effect.

Because social scientists and planners have a penchant for unitary definitions that cover all contingencies, there is still much discussion of what makes for a good neighborhood. Our approach suggests that the penchant should be carefully restrained. It is not necessarily true, for example, that a vital neighborhood is one that supplies a strong sense of social cohesion or reinforces personal identity with the group. In fact many people want neighborhoods where free choice in association and even anonymity are cherished. That kind of neighborhood, usually urban, is no less a neighborhood for its lack of social cohesion. Cohesion exacts its price in loss of personal freedom; freedom may be paid for in the coin of alienation and loneliness.

One pays the price for the neighborhood of one's choice. Making that choice possible is the function of the *idea* of neighborhood as it is embodied in many actual neighborhoods. It is not possible to create the benefits of each kind of neighborhood in every neighborhood. One cannot devise a compromise between the cohesion of a New England small town and the anonymity of the East Village without destroying both options.

Nor is it necessarily true that progress is marked by movement from the neighborhood of cohesion to the neighborhood of elective choice. Members of the cultural elite, who have strong influence on the metaphors by which public policy is designed, frequently feel they have escaped from the parochialisms of the former type of neighborhood. Such escapes are one source of the continuing vitality of great cities, but this idea of liberation should not be made normative. The Upper West Side of New York City, for example, the neighborhood of so many literary, academic, and political persons, has its own forms of parochialism, its taboos and restrictions, approved beliefs and behavior patterns. The urban sophisticate's conformity to the values of individual self-fulfillment and tolerance can be as intolerant of the beliefs and behavior nurtured in the community centered in the St. Stanislaus American Legion branch of Hamtramck, Michigan, as the people of Hamtramck are intolerant of what is called liberation on the Upper West Side.

Karl Marx wrote tellingly of "the idiocy of village life." Important to our approach, however, is the recognition that what looks like idiocy may in fact be a kind of complexity with which we cannot cope or do not wish to be bothered. That is, the movement from the community of cohesion to cosmopolitanism, from village to urban neighborhood, is not necessarily a movement from the simple to the complex. In fact, those who move toward the cosmopolitan may be simplifying their lives by freeing themselves from the tangled associations—family, church, club, and so forth—that dominate village life. It is probably easier for an outsider to become a person of political and social consequence in New York City than in most small towns. In a large city almost everyone is an outsider by definition. To put it another way, in the world of urban emigrés there are enough little worlds so that everyone can be an insider somewhere. Against the urban and universalizing biases of much social thought, the mediating structures paradigm requires that we take seriously the structures, values, and habits by which people order their lives in neighborhoods, wherever those neighborhoods may be, and no matter whether they are cohesive or individualistic, elective or hereditary.

10

There is no inherent superiority in or inevitable movement toward the neighborhood whose life gravitates around the liberal Democratic club rather than around the parish church or union hall. The goal of public policy should be to sustain the diversity of neighborhoods in which people can remain and to which they can move in accord with what "fits" their self-understanding and their hopes for those about whom they care most.

The empowerment of people in neighborhoods is hardly the answer to all our social problems. Neighborhoods empowered to impose their values upon individual behavior and expression can be both coercive and cruel. Government that transcends neighborhoods must intervene to protect elementary human rights. Here again, however, the distinction between public and private spheres is critically important. In recent years an unbalanced emphasis upon individual rights has seriously eroded the community's power to sustain its democratically determined values in the public sphere. It is ironic, for example, to find people who support landmark commissions that exercise aesthetic censorship—for example, by forbidding owners of landmark properties to change so much as a step or a bay window without legal permission—and who, at the same time, oppose public control of pornography, prostitution, gambling, and other "victimless crimes" that violate neighborhood values more basic than mere aesthetics. In truth, a strong class factor is involved in this apparent contradiction. Houses in neighborhoods that are thought to be part of our architectural heritage are typically owned by people to whom values such as architectural heritage are important. These are usually not the people whose neighborhoods are assaulted by pornography, prostitution, and drug trafficking. In short, those who have power can call in the police to reinforce their values while the less powerful cannot.

This individualistic and neighborhood-destroying bias is reinforced by court judgments that tend to treat all neighborhoods alike. That is, the legal tendency is to assume that there is a unitary national community rather than a national community composed of thousands of communities. Thus, the people of Kokomo, Indiana, must accept public promotions of pornography, for instance, because such promotions are protected by precedents established in Berkeley, California, or in Times Square. It is just barely arguable that the person who wants to see a live sex show in downtown Kokomo would be denied a constitutional right were such shows locally prohibited. It is a great deal clearer that the people of Kokomo are now denied the right to determine democratically the character of the community in

11

which they live. More careful distinctions are required if we are to stay the rush toward a situation in which civil liberties are viewed as the enemy of communal values and law itself is pitted against the power of people to shape their own lives. Such distinctions must reflect a greater appreciation of the differences between public and private behavior.

One reason for the present confusion about individual and communal rights has been the unreflective extension of policies deriving from America's racial dilemma to other areas where they are neither practicable nor just. That is, as a nation, and after a long, tortuous, and continuing agony, we have solemnly covenanted to disallow any public regulation that discriminates on the basis of race. That national decision must in no way be compromised. At the same time, the singularity of America's racial history needs to be underscored. Public policy should be discriminating about discriminations. Discrimination is the essence of particularism and particularism is the essence of pluralism. The careless expansion of antidiscrimination rulings in order to appease every aggrieved minority or individual will have two certain consequences: first, it will further erode local communal authority and, second, it will trivialize the historic grievances and claims to justice of America's racial minorities.

In terms of communal standards and sanctions, deviance always exacts a price. Indeed, without such standards, there can be no such thing as deviance. Someone who engages in public and deviant behavior in, say, Paducah, Kentucky, can pay the social price of deviance, can persuade his fellow citizens to accept his behavior, or can move to New York City. He should not be able to call in the police to prevent the people of Paducah from enforcing their values against his behavior. (Obviously, we are not referring to the expression of unpopular political or religious views, which, like proscriptions against racial discrimination, is firmly protected by national law and consensus.) The city—variously viewed as the cesspool of wickedness or the zone of liberation—has historically been the place of refuge for the insistently deviant. It might be objected that our saying "he can move to the city" sounds like the "love it or leave it" argument of those who opposed anti-war protesters in the last decade. The whole point, however, is the dramatic difference between a nation and a neighborhood. One is a citizen of a nation and lays claim to the rights by which that nation is constituted. Within that nation there are numerous associations such as neighborhoods—more or less freely chosen—and membership in those associations is usually related to affinity. This nation is constituted as

12

an exercise in pluralism, as the *unum* within which myriad *plures* are sustained. If it becomes national policy to make the public values of Kokomo or Salt Lake City indistinguishable from those of San Francisco or New Orleans, we have as a nation abandoned the social experiment symbolized by the phrase "E Pluribus Unum."

Viewed in this light, the *national* purpose does not destroy but aims at strengthening particularity, including the particularity of the neighborhood. It would be naive, however, to deny 'that there are points at which the *unum* and the *plures* are in conflict. It is patently the case, for example, that one of the chief determinants in shaping neighborhoods, especially in urban areas, is the racism that marks American life. The problem, of course, is that racial discrimination is often inseparable from other discriminations based upon attitudes, behavior patterns, and economic disparities. One may sympathize with those who are so frustrated in their effort to overcome racial injustice that they advocate policies aimed at wiping out every vestige and consequence of past racial discrimination. In fact, however, such leveling policies are relentlessly resisted by almost all Americans, including the black and the poor who, rightly or wrongly, see their interests attached to a system of rewards roughly associated with "free enterprise." The more practicable and, finally, the more just course is advanced by those who advocate massive public policy support for neighborhood development as development is defined by the people in the neighborhoods. As people in poor neighborhoods realize more of the "middle class" goals to which they undoubtedly aspire, racial discrimination will be reduced or at least will be more readily isolated than now and thus more easily reachable by legal proscription. The achievement of the poor need not mean that achievers move out of poor neighborhoods, thus leaving behind a hard core of more "ghettoized" residents. It is often overlooked, for example, that many middle-class and wealthy blacks *choose* to live in Harlem, creating "good neighborhoods" within an area often dismissed as hopeless. The dynamics of such community maintenance deserve more careful study and wider appreciation.

The pervasiveness of racial prejudice among whites means that blacks cannot depend upon economic mobility alone to gain freedom in choosing where to live and how to live. The communications media, churches, schools, government, and other institutions with some moral authority must continue and indeed intensify efforts to educate against racial bias. Where instances of racial discrimination can be reasonably isolated from other factors, they must be rigorously prosecuted and punished. It remains true, however, that economics and the values associated with middle-class status are key to overcoming racism. The public policy focus must therefore be on the development of the communities where people are. To the objection that this means locking the black and poor into present patterns of segregation, it must be answered that nothing would so surely lock millions of black Americans into hopelessness as making progress contingent upon a revolution in American racial attitudes or in the economic system. It is not too much to say that the alternative to neighborhood development is either neglect or revolution. Neglect is morally intolerable and, in the long run, probably too costly to the whole society to be viable even if it were acceptable morally. Revolution is so utterly improbable that it would be an unconscionable cruelty to encourage the poor to count on it.

The current attack on the existing pattern of housing and zoning regulations is, we believe, wrongheaded in several respects. Unless such regulations are almost totally dismantled, the attack is hardly worth pressing; and, if they are dismantled, the likely result would be great injustice to the poor whom the changes were designed to benefit and to the nonpoor who would certainly resist such changes. Those who propose to overcome poverty by spreading the poor more evenly seldom consider whether the burden of poverty might not be increased by virtue of its stark contrast with the affluence it would then be forced to live with. Even were it logistically and politically possible to distribute South Chicago's welfare families throughout the metropolitan area, it is doubtful their lot would be improved by living in projects, large or small, next to the $80,000 homes of the more prosperous suburbs. The people who live in those suburbs now do so quite deliberately in order to get away from the social problems associated with poverty—and, in a fashion too often related to racism, to get away from the minorities most commonly associated with those problems. It is one thing to make white Americans feel guilty about racism; it is quite another (and both wrong and futile) to make them feel guilty about their middle-class values— values also enthusiastically endorsed by the poor. These considerations aside, the great wrong in proposals to overcome poverty by dispersing the poor is that they would deprive the poor, whether black or white, of their own communities. Again, the proposition implicit in so much well-intended social advocacy—the proposition that an all-black neighborhood or all-black school is of necessity inferior—is aptly described as reverse racism. To the extent the proposition is internalized by the black poor, it also tends to become a self-fulfilling prophecy.

14

In sum, with respect to the connection between neighborhood and race, we would draw a sharp distinction between a society of *proscription* and a society of *prescription*. We have as a society covenanted to proscribe racial discrimination in the public realm. That proscription must be tirelessly implemented, no matter how frustrating the efforts at implementation sometimes are. But it is quite another matter to pursue policies of *prescription* in which government agencies prescribe quotas and balances for the redistribution of people and wealth. Pushed far enough, the second course invites revolutionary reaction, and it would almost certainly be revolution from the right. Pushed as far as it is now being pushed, it is eroding community power, distracting from the tasks of neighborhood development, and alienating many Americans from the general direction of domestic public policy.

If it is to make a real difference, neighborhood development should be distinguished from programs of decentralization. From Honolulu to Newton, Massachusetts, the last ten years have witnessed an explosion of neighborhood councils, "little city halls" dispersed through urban areas, and the like. Again, the decentralized operation of megastructures is not the same thing as the creation of vital mediating structures—indeed, it can be quite the opposite. Decentralization can give the people in the neighborhoods the feeling that they are being listened to, and even participating, but it has little to do with development and governance unless it means the reality as well as the sensations of power. Neighborhood governance exists when— in areas such as education, health services, law enforcement, and housing regulation—the people democratically determine what is in the interest of their own chosen life styles and values.

Many different streams flow into the current enthusiasms for neighborhood government. Sometimes the neighborhood government movement is dubbed "the new Jeffersonianism." After two centuries of massive immigration and urbanization, we cannot share Jefferson's bucolic vision of rural and small-town America, just as we do not indulge the re-medievalizing fantasies associated in some quarters with the acclaim for smallness. We believe the premise on which to devise public policy is that the parameters of modern, industrial, technological society are set for the foreseeable future. Our argument is not against modernity but in favor of exploring the ways in which modernity can be made more humane. With respect to neighborhood government, for example, it was widely assumed fifty and more years ago that modernity required the "rationalization" of urban polity. This was the premise of the "reform" and "good government" movements promoting the managerial, as distinct from partisan political, style of urban governance. The limitations of that approach are more widely recognized today.

It is recognized, for example, that the managerial model, however well-intended in many instances, served certain vested interests. Black writers and politicians have noted, and with some justice, an apparent racial component in the movement away from what some consider the irrationalities of local control. As urban populations become more black, some reformers put more emphasis upon regional planning and control, thus depriving blacks of their turn at wielding urban power. In 1976, during New York City's fiscal crisis, when more and more power was transferred to the state government, to the banks, and to Washington, it was widely and ruefully remarked that the power brokers were getting ready for the election of the first black or Puerto Rican mayor, who would be endowed with full authority to cut ceremonial ribbons.

In addition, there are today hundreds of thousands of public employees, politicians, planners, and theorists who have deep vested interest in maintaining the dike of "national organization" against what they allege is the threatening chaos of community control. The prospect of neighborhood government must be made to seem less threatening to these many dependents of centralization. Their legitimate interests must be accommodated if neighborhood government is to mature from a protest movement to a guiding metaphor of public policy. A distinction should be made, for example, between unionized professionals and professional unionists. The former need not be threatened by the role we propose for the neighborhood and other mediating structures in public policy. In fact many new opportunities might be opened for the exercise of truly professional imagination in greater responsiveness to the felt needs of people. With many more institutional players in the public realm, professionals could have greater choice and freedom for innovation. The protection of professional interests through unions and other associations need not be dependent upon the perpetuation of the monolithic managerial models for ordering society.

One factor sparking enthusiasm for community control and neighborhood government is the growing realization that localities may not be receiving a fair break when it comes to tax monies. That is, some studies suggest that even poor neighborhoods, after everything is taken into account, end up sending considerably more out of the neighborhood in taxes than is returned. We do not suggest that the income tax, for instance, should be administered locally.

16

It is reasonable to inquire, however, whether the tax-collecting function of the federal and state governments could not be maintained, while the spending function is changed to allow tax monies to be returned in a noncategorical way to the places where they were raised to begin with. Needless to say, this suggestion goes far beyond what is currently called revenue sharing. Nor does it ignore the fact that sizable funds are required for functions that transcend the purview of any neighborhood, such as transportation or defense. But again—focusing on activities of the kind carried on by the Department of Health, Education and Welfare (HEW)—it does imply that the people in communities know best what is needed for the maintenance and development of those communities.

If neighborhoods are to be key to public policy, governmental action is necessary to fund neighborhood improvement. As is well known, practices such as red-lining deteriorating neighborhoods are today very common. It may be that there is no effective way to force private financial institutions to make monies available for home improvement and other investments in "ghetto" neighborhoods. Without a direct assault upon the free enterprise system, the possibilities of evasion and subterfuge in order to invest money where it is safest or most profitable are almost infinite. To strengthen the mediating role of neighborhoods we need to look to new versions of the Federal Housing Administration assistance programs that played such a large part in the burgeoning suburbs after World War II. Such programs can, we believe, be developed to sustain and rehabilitate old communities, as they have been used to build new ones. The idea of urban homesteading, for example, although afflicted with corruption and confusion in recent years, is a move in the right direction. At a very elementary level, property tax regulations should be changed to encourage rather than discourage home improvement. Especially in large metropolitan areas, granting the most generous tax "breaks" might in the not-so-long run yield more revenue than the current system, especially since in many places the abandonment of buildings means that present taxation levels yield little. In short, the tax structure should be changed in every way that encourages the tenant to become a homeowner and the landlord to improve his property.

Neighborhoods will also be strengthened as people in the neighborhood assume more and more responsibility for law enforcement, especially in the effort to stem the tide of criminal terrorism. In this area, too, we have become so enamored of professionalism and so fearful of vigilantism that we have forgotten that community values

17

are only operative when the people in the community act upon them. We should not limit ourselves to thinking about how communities might control conventional police operations and personnel. Rather, we should examine the informal "law enforcement agents" that exist in every community—the woman who runs the local candy store, the people who walk their dogs, or the old people who sit on park benches or observe the streets from their windows. This means new approaches to designing "defensible space" in housing, schools, and the like. It certainly suggests the need to explore the part-time employment, through public funding, of parents and others who would police schools and other public spaces. We have been increasingly impressed, in conversation with people knowledgeable about law enforcement, with the point that there are probably few fields of law enforcement requiring the kind of metropolitan, comprehensive, and professional police force which have come to be taken for granted as an urban necessity. The fact is that there is probably no neighborhood in which the overwhelming majority of residents do not wish to see the laws enforced. Yet the residents feel impotent and therefore the neighborhoods often are impotent in doing anything about crime. The ways in which public policies have fostered that feeling of impotence must be examined, and alternatives to such policies found.

Finally, no discussion of neighborhood can ignore the homogenizing role of the mass communications media in creating a common culture. We suspect, and frankly hope, that the influence of the mass media in destroying the particularisms of American society is frequently overestimated. Television certainly is a tremendous force in creating something like a national discourse regarding current affairs and even values. We do not advocate the dismantling of the national networks. We do propose, however, that it be public policy to open up many unused channels, now technically available, for the use of regional, ethnic, and elective groups of all sorts. Similarly, taxation policies, postal regulations, and other factors should be reexamined with a view toward sustaining neighborhood newspapers and other publications.

All of which is to say that the goal of making and keeping life human, of sustaining a people-sized society, depends upon our learning again that parochialism is not a nasty word. Like the word parish, it comes from the Greek, *para* plus *oikos*, the place next door. Because we all want some choice and all have a great stake in the place where we live, it is in the common interest to empower our own places and the places next door.

III. FAMILY

There are places, especially in urban areas, where life styles are largely detached from family connections. This is, one hopes, good for those who choose it. Certainly such life styles add to the diversity, the creativity, even the magic, of the city. But since a relatively small number of people inhabit these areas, it would be both foolish and undemocratic to take such life styles as guidelines for the nation. For most Americans, neighborhood and community are closely linked to the family as an institution.

The family may be in crisis in the sense that it is undergoing major changes of definition, but there is little evidence that it is in decline. High divorce rates, for example, may indicate not decline but rising expectations in what people look for in marriage and family life. The point is underscored by high remarriage rates. It is noteworthy that the counterculture, which is so critical of the so-called bourgeois family, uses the terminology of family for its new social constructions, as do radical feminists pledged to "sisterhood." For most Americans, the evidence is that involvement in the bourgeois family, however modified, will endure.

Of course, modernization has already had a major impact on the family. It has largely stripped the family of earlier functions in the areas of education and economics, for example. But in other ways, modernization has made the family more important than ever before. It is the major institution within the private sphere, and thus for many people the most valuable thing in their lives. Here they make their moral commitments, invest their emotions, plan for the future, and perhaps even hope for immortality.

There is a paradox here. On the one hand, the megastructures of government, business, mass communications, and the rest have left room for the family to be the autonomous realm of individual aspiration and fulfillment. This room is by now well secured in the legal definitions of the family. At the same time, the megastructures persistently infringe upon the family. We cannot and should not eliminate these infringements entirely. After all, families exist in a common society. We can, however, take positive measures to protect and foster the family institution, so that it is not defenseless before the forces of modernity.

This means public recognition of the family *as an institution.* It is not enough to be concerned for individuals more or less incidentally related to the family as institution. Public recognition of the family as an institution is imperative because every society has an

inescapable interest in how children are raised, how values are trans-
mitted to the next generation. Totalitarian regimes have tried—un-
successfully to date—to supplant the family in this function. Democratic societies dare not try if they wish to remain democratic. Indeed
they must resist every step, however well intended, to displace or
weaken the family institution.

Public concern for the family is not antagonistic to concern for
individual rights. On the contrary, individuals need strong families
if they are to grow up and remain rooted in a strong sense of identity
and values. Weak families produce uprooted individuals, unsure of
their direction and therefore searching for some authority. They are
ideal recruits for authoritarian movements inimical to democratic
society.

Commitment to the family institution can be combined, although
not without difficulty, with an emphatically libertarian view that pro-
tects the private lives of adults against public interference of any
kind. Public interest in the family is centered on children, not adults;
it touches adults insofar as they are in charge of children. The public
interest is institutional in character. That is, the state is to view
children as members of a family. The sovereignty of the family over
children has limits—as does any sovereignty in the modern world—
and these limits are already defined in laws regarding abuse, criminal
neglect, and so on. The onus of proof, however, must be placed on
policies or laws that foster state interference rather than on those
that protect family autonomy. In saying this we affirm what has
been the major legal tradition in this country.

Conversely, we oppose policies that expose the child directly to
state intervention, without the mediation of the family. We are
skeptical about much current discussion of children's rights—especially when such rights are asserted *against* the family. Children do
have rights, among which is the right to a functionally strong family.
When the rhetoric of children's rights means transferring children
from the charge of families to the charge of coteries of experts ("We
know what is best for the children"), that rhetoric must be suspected
of cloaking vested interests—ideological interests, to be sure, but,
also and more crudely, interest in jobs, money, and power.

Our preference for the parents over the experts is more than
a matter of democratic conviction—and does not ignore the existence
of relevant and helpful expertise. It is a bias based upon the simple,
but often overlooked, consideration that virtually all parents love
their children. Very few experts love, or can love, most of the children
in their care. Not only is that emotionally difficult, but expertise

generally requires a degree of emotional detachment. In addition, the parent, unike the expert, has a long-term, open-ended commitment to the individual child. Thus the parent, almost by definition, is way ahead of the expert in sheer knowledge of the child's character, history, and needs. The expert, again by definition, relates to the child within general and abstract schemata. Sometimes the schemata fit, but very often they do not.

We have no intention of glorifying the bourgeois family. Foster parents, lesbians and gays, liberated families, or whatever—all can do the job *as long as* they provide children the loving and the permanent structure that traditional families have typically provided. Indeed, virtually any structure is better for children than what experts or the state can provide.

Most modern societies have in large part disfranchised the family in the key area of education. The family becomes, at best, an auxiliary agency to the state, which at age five or six coercively (compulsory school laws) and monopolistically (for the most part) takes over the child's education. Of course there are private schools, but here class becomes a powerful factor. Disfranchisement falls most heavily on lower-income parents who have little say in what happens to their children in school. This discrimination violates a fundamental human right, perhaps the most fundamental human right—the right to make a world for one's children.

Our purpose is not to deprive upper-income families of the choices they have. The current assault on private schools in Britain (there called public schools) is not a happy example. Our purpose is to give those choices to those who do not now have decision-making power. When some are freezing while others enjoy bright fires, the solution is not to extinguish all fires equally but to provide fires for those who have none.

There is yet a further class discrimination in education. By birth or social mobility, the personnel of the education establishment are upper middle class, and this is reflected in the norms, the procedures, and the very cultural climate of that establishment. This means the child who is not of an upper-middle-class family is confronted by an alien milieu from his or her first day at school. In part this may be inevitable. The modern world is bourgeois and to succeed in a bourgeois world means acquiring bourgeois skills and behavior patterns. We do not suggest, as some do, that the lower-class child is being culturally raped when taught correct English. But there are many other, sometimes unconscious, ways in which the education establishment systematically disparages ways of life other than those of the upper middle class. Yet these disparaged ways of life are precisely the ways in which parents of millions of American children live. Thus schools teach contempt for the parents and, ultimately, self-contempt.

In a few metropolitan areas, the education establishment has responded to these problems, sometimes creatively. But monopolies endowed with coercive powers do not change easily. The best way to induce change is to start breaking up the monopoly—to empower people *to shop elsewhere*. We trust the ability of low-income parents to make educational decisions more wisely than do the professionals who now control their children's education. To deny this ability is the worst class bias of all, and in many instances it is racism as well.

To affirm empowerment against tutelage, irrespective of economic or social status, is hardly a wildly radical position. That it may seem so to some is a measure of the elitist and essentially antidemocratic effects of the bureaucratization and professionalization of American society.

Against the politics of resentment, empowerment is not a zero-sum game. That is, lower-income people can be enfranchised without disfranchising or impoverishing the better off. But this process does assume a lower limit of poverty beyond which efforts at empowerment are futile. Any humane and effective social policy must place a floor of decency under everyone in the society. The relative merits of income maintenance programs—guaranteed income, negative income tax, and so forth—are beyond the scope of this essay, but the whole argument assumes that a floor of decency must be established. Aside from moral imperatives, such a floor can strengthen mediating structures, notably here poor families, by helping them break out of present patterns of dependency upon a confused and confusing welfare system.

The implications of our policy concept may be clarified by looking briefly at three currently discussed issues—education vouchers, day care, and the care of the handicapped. The idea of education vouchers has been around for a while and has had its ups and downs, but it remains one of the most intriguing possibilities for radical reform in the area of education. In this proposal, public funding of education shifts from disbursement to schools to disbursement to individuals. Parents (or, at a certain age, their children) choose the schools where they will cash in their vouchers, the schools then being reimbursed by the state. Essentially the proposal applies the paradigm of the GI Bill to younger students at earlier periods of education. This proposal would break the coercive monopoly of the present education system and empower individuals in relating to the mega-structures of bureaucracy and professionalism, with special benefits going to lower-income people. In addition, it would enhance the diversity of American life by fostering particularist communities of value—whether of life style, ideology, religion, or ethnicity. And all this without increasing, and maybe decreasing, costs to the taxpayer since, at least at the primary levels of education, the evidence suggests that economies of scale do not operate.

Politically, education vouchers have advocates on the right and on the left, notably Milton Friedman and Christopher Jencks, respectively. The chief difference is whether vouchers should be basic or total—that is, whether upper-income parents should have the right to supplement vouchers with their own money. Friedman says they should because they have a right to the benefits of their taxes without surrendering the free use of their income. Jencks, for egalitarian reasons, says they should not. On this we incline toward Friedman's position for two reasons: first, the purpose of schools is to educate children, not to equalize income; and second, as stated before, lower-income people can be empowered without penalizing others. Needless to say, the second consideration has much to do with the political salability of education vouchers and, indeed, of the mediating structures paradigm in other policy areas.

There have been limited experiments with the voucher idea within existing public school systems (Seattle; Alum Rock, California; and Gary, Indiana). The results are still being analyzed, but already certain cautions have been raised. An urgent caution is that under no circumstances should vouchers be used to subsidize schools that practice racial exclusion. Another caution is that vouchers are not given a fair trial unless the experiment includes schools outside the public school system. (Of course this raises certain church-state considerations, and we will address them in the next section.)

Among other questions still unanswered: Should vouchers be uniform or graded by income? Should the state insist on a core curriculum, and, if so, should compliancy be ensured by inspection or by examination? Should present methods of teacher certification be extended to schools now considered private? What are the other implications of, in effect, making all schools public schools? And, of course, what would be the effect of a voucher system on teachers unions? Although the unions have tended to be antagonistic to the idea so far, we believe that both bread-and-butter interests and professional interests can be secured, and in some ways better secured than now, within a voucher framework.

Obviously we cannot address all these questions here. We are struck, however, by the fact that almost all the objections to the voucher idea have been on grounds *other than educational*. And education, after all, is what schools are supposed to be about.

Turning to our second example, we note that day care has become a public issue, as more and more mothers of small children have entered the labor force and as many people, spurred by the feminist movement, have begun to claim that working mothers have a right to public services designed to meet their special needs. Both factors are likely to continue, making day care a public issue for the foreseeable future.

Three positions on national day-care policy can be discerned at present. One is that the government should, quite simply, stay out of this area. Financially, it is said, any program will be enormously costly and, ideologically, the government should refrain from intruding itself so massively into the area of early childhood. Another position endorses a federally funded, comprehensive child-care system attached to the public schools. This is the view of the American Federation of Teachers. A third position is much like the second, except that the national program would be less closely linked to the public school system. (This position was embodied in the Mondale-Brademas bill which President Ford vetoed in 1976.) As in the Head Start program, this plan would work through prime sponsors. These sponsors could be private or public, voluntary associations, neighborhood groups, or simply parents getting together to run a day-care center—the only condition being that sponsors be nonprofit in character.

It should come as no surprise that we favor the third position. We do so because there is a real need and because the need should be met in a way that is as inexpensive and as unintrusive as possible. The mediating structures concept is ideally suited to the latter purpose and may also advance the former. As to the second position mentioned above, we are sympathetic to the teachers union's desire for new jobs in a period of educational retrenchment. But, again, providing jobs should not be the purpose of education and child care.

The voucher approach can be the more readily used in day care since there are not as yet in this area the powerful vested interests so firmly established in primary and secondary education. Vouchers would facilitate day-care centers that are small, not professionalized, under the control of parents, and therefore highly diversified. State intervention should be strictly limited to financial accountability and to safety and health standards (which, perhaps not incidentally, are absurdly unrealistic in many states). Considerable funds can be saved through this approach since it is virtually certain that economies of scale do not apply to day-care centers. Imaginative proposals should be explored, such as the use of surrogate grandparents—which, incidentally, would offer meaningful employment to the growing numbers of elderly persons in our society. (We realize that we argued above that employment should not be the purpose of education, but presumably teachers *can* do something other than teach school, while surrogate grandparents may be restricted to grandparenting.)

The third issue mentioned is care of the handicapped. An important case in this area is the so-called special child—special children being those who, for a broad range of nonphysical reasons, are handicapped in their educational development. The field of special education has grown rapidly in recent years and many of its problems (medical and educational as well as legal) are outside our present scope. One problem within our scope is the recurring choice between institutionalizing the severely handicapped and dealing with their problems within the family setting.

Apart from the inability of the normal family to deal with some severe handicaps, the trend toward institutionalization has been propelled by considerations such as the convenience of parents, the vested interests of professionals, and the alleged therapeutic superiority of institutional settings. Because the therapeutic claims of these institutions have been shown to be highly doubtful, and because institutional care is immensely expensive, innovative thinking today moves toward using the family as a therapeutic context *as much as possible.* This means viewing the professional as *ancillary* to, rather than as a substitute for, the resources of the family. It may mean paying families to care for a handicapped child, enabling a parent to work less or not at all, or to employ others. Such an approach would almost certainly reduce costs in caring for the handicapped. More important, and this can be amply demonstrated, the best therapeutic results are obtained when children remain in their families—or, significantly, in institutional settings that imitate family life. (We will not repeat what we said earlier about the relative merits of love and expertise.) And, of course, there is no reason why this proposal could not be extended to the care of handicapped adults.

Again, we are well aware of current misgivings about the traditional family, misgivings pressed by feminists but not by feminists alone. As far as adults are concerned, we favor maximizing choices about life styles. The principal public policy interest in the family concerns children, not adults. This interest is common to all societies, but in democratic society there is an additional and urgent interest in fostering socialization patterns and values that allow individual autonomy. That interest implies enhanced protection of the family in relation to the state, and it implies trusting people to be responsible for their own children in a world of their own making.

IV. CHURCH

Religious institutions form by far the largest network of voluntary associations in American society. Yet, for reasons both ideological and historical, their role is frequently belittled or totally overlooked in discussions of social policy. Whatever may be one's attitude to organized religion, this blind spot must be reckoned a serious weakness in much thinking about public policy. The churches and synagogues of America can no more be omitted from responsible social analysis than can big labor, business corporations, or the communications media. Not only are religious institutions significant "players" in the public realm, but they are singularly important to the way people order their lives and values at the most local and concrete levels of their existence. Thus they are crucial to understanding family, neighborhood, and other mediating structures of empowerment.

The view that the public sphere is synonymous with the government or the formal polity of the society has been especially effective in excluding religion from considerations of public policy. We shall return to some of the church/state controversies that have reflected and perpetuated this view; but for the moment it should be obvious that our whole proposal aims at a complex and nuanced understanding of the public realm that includes many "players" other than the state. Also, much modern social thought deriving from Enlightenment traditions has operated on one or two assumptions that tend to minimize the role of religion. The first assumption is that education and modernization make certain the decline of allegiance to institutional religion. That is, there is thought to be an inevitable connection between modernization and secularization. The second assumption is that, even if religion continues to flourish, it deals purely with the private sphere of life and is therefore irrelevant to public policy. Both assumptions need to be carefully reexamined.

The evidence, at least in America, does not support the hypothesis of the inevitable decline of religion. Although the decline is perennially announced—its announcement being greeted with both cheers and lamentations—it is likely that religion is at least as institutionally intact as some other major institutions (such as, for example, higher education). It is worth noting that in recent years the alleged decline of religion has been measured by comparison with the so-called religious boom of the late 1950s. The comparison with that unprecedented period of institutional growth offers a very skewed perspective. But, even when the vitality of religion is measured by that misleading comparison, it is notable that in the past few years the indexes are again on the upswing. Church attendance, claimed affiliation, financial contributions, and other indicators all suggest that whatever decline there was from the apex of the late 1950s has now stopped or been reversed. It is perhaps relevant to understanding American society to note that on any given Sunday there are probably more people in churches than the total number of people who attend professional sports events in a whole year—or to note that there are close to 500,000 local churches and synagogues voluntarily supported by the American people.

This is not the place for a detailed discussion of various secularization theories. We are keenly aware of the need to distinguish between institutions of religion and the dynamic of religion as such in society. Let it suffice that our approach raises a strong challenge to the first assumption mentioned above, namely, that in the modern world allegiance to institutional religion must perforce decline. Public policies based upon that highly questionable, if not patently false, assumption will continue to be alienated from one of the most vital dimensions in the lives of many millions of Americans.

The second assumption—that religion deals purely with the private sphere and is therefore irrelevant to public policy—must also be challenged. Although specifically religious activities have been largely privatized, the first part of the proposition overlooks the complex ways in which essentially religious values infiltrate and influence our public thought. But even to the extent that the first part of the proposition is true, it does not follow that religion is therefore irrelevant to public policy. The family, for example, is intimately involved in the institution of religion, and since the family is one of the prime mediating structures (perhaps the prime one), this makes the church urgently relevant to public policy. Without falling into the trap of politicizing all of life, our point is that structures such as family, church, and neighborhood are all public institutions in the sense that they must be taken seriously in the ordering of the polity.

The church (here meaning all institutions of religion) is important not only to the family but also to families and individuals in neighborhoods and other associations. For example, the black community, both historically and at present, cannot be understood apart from the black church. Similarly, the much discussed ethnic community is in large part religiously defined, as are significant parts of American Jewry (sometimes, but not always, subsumed under the phenomenon of ethnicity). And of course the role of religion in small towns or rural communities needs no elaboration. In none of these instances should the religious influence be viewed as residual. Few institutions have demonstrated and continue to demonstrate perduring power comparable to that of religion. It seems that influence is residual only to the extent that the bias of secularizing culture and politics is determined to act as though it is residual. Again, these observations seem to us to be true quite apart from what we may or may not *wish* the influence of religion to be in American society. We are convinced that there is a profoundly antidemocratic prejudice in public policy discourse that ignores the role of religious institutions in the lives of most Americans.

In the public policy areas most relevant to this discussion—health, social welfare, education, and so on—the historical development of programs, ideas, and institutions is inseparable from the church. In some parts of the country, notably in the older cities of the Northeast, the great bulk of social welfare services function under religious auspices. For reasons to be discussed further in the next section, the religious character of these service agencies is being fast eroded. Where government agencies are not directly taking over areas previously serviced by religious institutions, such institutions are being turned into quasi-governmental agencies through the powers of funding, certification, licensing, and the like. The loss of religious and cultural distinctiveness is abetted also by the dynamics of professionalization within the religious institutions and by the failure of the churches either to support their agencies or to insist that public policy respect their distinctiveness. The corollary to the proposition that government responsibilities must be governmentally implemented —a proposition we challenge—is that public is the opposite of sectarian. In public policy discourse sectarian is usually used as a term of opprobrium for anything religious. We contend that this usage and the biases that support it undermine the celebration of distinctiveness essential to social pluralism.

The homogenizing consequences of present patterns of funding, licensing, and certification are intensified by tax policies that have a "chilling effect" upon the readiness of religious institutions to play their part in the public realm. The threatened loss of tax exemption because of excessive "political activity" is a case in point. Even more ominous is the developing notion of tax expenditures (on which more in Section V). Most recently what has been called tax reform has aimed at driving a wedge between churches as such and their church-related auxiliaries, making the latter subject to disclosure, accounta bility, and therefore greater control by the state. These directions are, we believe, fundamentally wrongheaded. Pushed far enough, they will likely provoke strong reaction from a public that will not countenance what is perceived as an attack on religion. But public policy decision makers should not wait for that reaction to supply a corrective to present tendencies. It is precisely in the interest of public policy to advance a positive approach to the church as a key mediating structure.

Obviously all these questions touch on the complex of issues associated with separation of church and state. We believe, together with many scholars of jurisprudence, that the legal situation of church/state questions is today bogged down in conceptual confusions and practical contradictions. "The wall of separation between church and state" (Jefferson's phrase, not the Constitution's) is a myth long overdue for thorough rethinking. We are deeply committed to the religion clauses of the First Amendment. They should not be understood, however, as requiring absolute separationism; such absolute separationism is theoretically inconceivable and practically contrary to the past and present interaction of church and state. It is yet another of those grand abstractions that have had such a debilitating effect upon the way society's institutions relate to one another and upon the way in which people actually order their own lives.

In brief, "no establishment of religion" should mean that no religious institution is favored by the state over other religious institutions. "Free exercise of religion" should mean that no one is forced to practice or profess any religion against his will. Where there is neither favoritism nor coercion by the state there is no violation of the separation of church and state. While the subject is more complicated than suggested here, and while the courts will no doubt take time to disentangle themselves from the confusions into which they have been led, it is to be hoped that public policy will, in general, more nearly approximate "the Kurland rule" (named after Philip Kurland of the University of Chicago), namely, that if a policy furthers a legitimate secular purpose it is a matter of legal indifference whether or not that policy employs religious institutions. Clearly, this has far-ranging implications in the areas of education, child care, and social services generally.

The danger today is not that the churches or any one church will take over the state. The much more real danger is that the state will take over the functions of the church, except for the most narrowly construed definition of religion limited to worship and religious instruction. It is not alarmist but soberly necessary to observe that the latter has been the totalitarian pattern of modern states, whether of the left or of the right. Pluralism, including religious pluralism, is one of the few strong obstacles to that pattern's success. While those who advance this pattern may often do so inadvertently, it would be naive to ignore the fact that many of them—sundry professionals, bureaucrats, politicians—have a deep vested interest in such state expansion. The interest is not only ideological, although that is no doubt the primary interest in many cases; it is also and very practically an interest in jobs and power.

From the beginning, we have emphasized the importance of mediating structures in generating and maintaining values. We have already discussed the function of the family in this connection. Within the family, and between the family and the larger society, the church is a primary agent for bearing and transmitting the operative values of our society. This is true not only in the sense that most Americans identify their most important values as being religious in character, but also in the sense that the values that inform our public discourse are inseparably related to specific religious traditions. In the absence of the church and other mediating structures that articulate these values, the result is not that the society is left without operative values; the result is that the state has an unchallenged monopoly on the generation and maintenance of values. Needless to say, we would find this a very unhappy condition indeed.

With respect to our minimalist proposition, that public policy should not undercut mediating structures, a number of implications become evident. Already mentioned are aspects of taxation and regulation, which we will treat more fully in the next section because they affect not only the church but all voluntary associations. More specific to religious institutions is the demand for "right to equal access," a notion that cannot help but undercut particularism. Here again we run into the problem of not being discriminating about discriminations or, to put it differently, of failing to distinguish between discrimination and discretion. It seems to us, for example, there is nothing wrong with an elderly Italian Roman Catholic woman wanting to live in a nursing home operated and occupied by Italian Roman Catholics. To challenge that most understandable desire seems to us, quite frankly, perverse. Yet challenged it is—indeed, it is made increasingly impossible—by depriving such a "sectarian" or "discriminatory" institution of public funds. The same obviously holds true for Methodists, atheists, Humanists, and Black Muslims. Public policy's legitimate secular purpose is to ensure that old people have proper care. It should also be public policy that such care be available as much as possible within the context that people desire for themselves and for those whom they care most about. Again, the unique proscription relevant to public policy is against racial discrimination. (To contend that, since there are few black Italian Roman Catholics or few white Black Muslims, this constitutes racial discrimination *in result* is the kind of absurd exercise in social abstraction that plagues too much policy thinking today.)

A most poignant instance of public policy's undercutting the mediating structure of religion is that of present litigation aimed at prohibiting adoption and foster-care agencies from employing a religious criterion. That is, it is proposed to outlaw agencies designed to serve Jewish, Protestant, or Catholic children, if those agencies receive public funds (which of course they do). The cruel and dehumanizing consequences of this are several. First, the parent putting a child up for adoption or surrendering a child to foster care is deprived of the most elementary say in how that child is to be reared. As mentioned in the last section, this is among the most basic of human rights and should not be denied except under the most pressing necessity, especially when one considers that the surrender of children to such agencies is not always entirely voluntary. Another consequence is that the motivation of paid and volunteer workers in such agencies is severely undercut. In many, if not most, instances that motivation is to live out and explicitly transmit religious conviction. Yet a further consequence, perhaps the most important, is that the child is deprived of religious training. This may well be construed as a denial of free exercise of religion. The state has no rightful authority to decide that this is not a serious deprivation. What is necessary to rearing the child should be left to those who bear the children and those who care for them. Except for cases of criminal neglect or other injury, the state should have no authority to intervene. Again, the legitimate secular purpose is that the children be cared for.

It might be objected that leaving such a wide range of social services to religious and other voluntary associations would mean that the many people who did not belong to such groups would go unserved. The objection is revealed as specious, however, when it is recalled that public funds would be made available to almost every conceivable kind of group so long as it were prepared to carry out the public policy purpose. Such agencies might espouse one religion, all religions, or none. Almost everyone belongs to some group that can, with public funds, facilitate public policy in the area of social services. In truth, if we are really concerned for those individuals who fall between the cracks, it is worth noting that the most anomic individuals in our society, the denizens of skid row for example, are cared for almost exclusively by voluntary associations, usually religious in character. Government bureaucracies—indeed, by definition, all bureaucracies—demonstrate little talent for helping the truly marginal who defy generalized categories. The Salvation Army needs no lessons from the state on how to be nonsectarian in its compassion for people. The raison d'être of the Salvation Army is seriously undercut, however, if its workers cannot preach to those to whom they minister.

Still on the minimalistic side of the proposition, the mediating structures paradigm opposes the growing trend toward legally enforced symbolic sterility in public space. A Christmas tree or Hanukkah lights on the town common is a good case in point. Voluntary prayer in public schools is another. "In God We Trust" inscribed on coins is another. Little things these may be, perhaps, but of myriad such little things the public ethos is formed. Reaching toward absurdity, a California court recently ruled that it was unconstitutional to have a state holiday on Good Friday. Presumably there is no objection to the previous Friday, since the secular purpose is to give another day off to state workers. But when secular purpose is combined with religious significance it is apparently beyond the pale of constitutionality.

Our proposition assumes that nobody has a right to be unaffected by the social milieu of which he or she is part. In Section II we touched on the tensions between individual and communal rights. If someone walks naked down Main Street, citizens now have the right to call in the police and have the offensive behavior stopped. Such regulations dealing with community values are of course undergoing change in many places. Change is a constant in the definition of community standards, and the authors probably tend to be more libertarian than most on the question of tolerating deviant behavior in public. The point here is that there must also be limits on the ability of individuals to call in the police to prevent behavior that is communally approved—for example, the Christmas tree on the town common. Nobody has a legal right not to encounter religious symbols in public places and thus to *impose his aversion* to such symbols on

32

the community that cherishes them. As long as public space is open to the full range of symbols cherished in that community, there is no question of one religion being "established" over another. Public policy is presently biased toward what might be called the symbolic nakedness of the town square. Again, social abstractions have resulted in antidemocratic consequences, antidemocratic because they deny the democratically determined will of the people to celebrate themselves—their culture and their beliefs—in public, and, just as important, consequences that are antidemocratic because they give to the state a monopoly on public space and on the values to be advanced in that space.

In a public housing project in Brooklyn a deal has been struck between the leaders of a Hassidic Jewish community and of the Hispanic community to rent apartments in a way that will concentrate both communities in a more or less intact manner. The deal is probably illegal, on grounds both of racial and religious discrimination. In this particular case, it is also eminently sensible and fair, and therefore ought to be legal. No one is hurt, unless it be the "strict separationist" and "geometrical integrationist" who may be offended by the violations of their abstractions. But they are not renting apartments in public housing. We stress "in this particular case"—because public policy, especially in the area of religion and communal values, should show more respect for particular cases.

Finally, on the maximalist side of our propositi should utilize mediating structures as much as feas tions spelled out throughout this essay apply also t proposal is that the institutions of religion should make their maximum contribution to the public i areas of social service and education, this means should be free to continue doing what they have hi

Again, and in accord with our maximalist prop increased public funding for the meeting of human range of policy areas; our particular contention i institutions, including religious institutions, be utilized as much as possible as the implementing agencies of policy goals. Contrary to some public policy and legal thinking today, such increased funding need not require an increase in governmental control and a consequent war on pluralism. With respect to the church and other mediating structures, the hope of the New Deal will be more nearly fulfilled when policies do not advance public compassion and responsibility at the price of conformity and repression.

V. VOLUNTARY ASSOCIATION

The discussion of the church leads logically to the subject of the voluntary association. Of course the church is—in addition to whatever else it may be—a voluntary association. But the category of voluntary association includes many other structures that can play a crucial mediating role in society.

There is a history of debate over what is meant by a voluntary association. For our present purposes, a voluntary association is a body of people who have voluntarily organized themselves in pursuit of particular goals. (Following common usage, we exclude business corporations and other primarily economic associations.) Important to the present discussion is the subject of volunteer service. Many voluntary associations have both paid and volunteer staffing. For our purposes, the crucial point is the free association of people for some collective purpose, the fact that they may pay some individuals for doing work to this end not being decisive.

At least since de Tocqueville the importance of voluntary associations in American democracy has been widely recognized. Voluntarism has flourished in America more than in any other Western society and it is reasonable to believe this may have something to do with American political institutions. Associations create statutes, elect officers, debate, vote courses of action, and otherwise serve as schools for democracy. However trivial, wrongheaded, or bizarre we may think the purpose of some associations to be, they nonetheless perform this vital function.

Apart from this political role, voluntary associations are enormously important for what they have actually done. Before the advent of the modern welfare state, almost everything in the realm of social services was under the aegis of voluntary associations, usually religious in character. Still today there are about 1,900 private colleges and universities, 4,600 private secondary schools, 3,600 voluntary hospitals, 6,000 museums, 1,100 orchestras, 5,500 libraries and no less than 29,000 nongovernmental welfare agencies. Of course not all of these are equally important as mediating structures. Orchestras and groups promoting stamp-collecting or the preservation of antique automobiles are, however important in other connections, outside our focus here. We are interested in one type within the vast array of voluntary associations—namely, associations that render social services relevant to recognized public responsibilities.

Assaults on voluntary associations come from several directions, from both the right and left of the political spectrum. Some condemn them as inefficient, corrupt, divisive, and even subversive. Many subscribe to the axiom that public services should not be under private control. From the far left comes the challenge that such associations supply mere palliatives, perpetuate the notion of charity, and otherwise manipulate people into acceptance of the status quo.

Such assaults are not merely verbal. They reflect a trend to establish a state monopoly over all organized activities that have to do with more than strictly private purposes. This trend has borne fruit in outright prohibition, in repressive taxation, and in the imposition of licensing and operating standards that have a punitive effect on nongovernmental agencies.

Of course there are instances of corruption and inefficiency in voluntary agencies. A comparison of governmental and nongovernmental social services on these scores, however, hardly supports the case for governmental monopoly. It should be obvious that government bureaucrats have a vested interest in maintaining and expanding government monopolies. Similarly, politicians have an interest in setting up services for which they can claim credit and over which they can exercise a degree of power. In short, social services in the modern welfare state are inescapably part of the political pork barrel.

Pork barrels may be necessary to political democracy. The problem confronting us arises when the vested interests in question use coercive state power to repress individual freedom, initiative, and social diversity. We are not impressed by the argument that this is necessary because voluntary associations often overlap with the functions of government agencies. Overlap may in fact provide creative competition, incentives for performance, and increased choice. But our more basic contention is against the notion that anything public must *ipso facto* be governmental. That notion is profoundly contrary to the American political tradition and is, in its consequences, antidemocratic. It creates clients of the state instead of free citizens. It stifles the initiative and responsibility essential to the life of the polity.

Our present problem is also closely linked with the trend toward professionalization. Whether in government or nongovernment agencies, professionals attack allegedly substandard services, and substandard generally means nonprofessional. Through organizations and lobbies, professionals increasingly persuade the state to legislate standards and certifications that hit voluntary associations hard, especially those given to employing volunteers. The end result is that the trend toward government monopoly operates in tandem with the trend toward professional monopoly over social services. The connection between such monopoly control and the actual quality of services delivered is doubtful indeed.

Professional standards are of course important in some areas. But they must be viewed with robust skepticism when expertise claims jurisdiction, as it were, over the way people run their own lives. Again, ordinary people are the best experts on themselves. Tutelage by certified experts is bad enough when exercised by persuasion—as, for example, when parents are so demoralized that they feel themselves incapable of raising their children without ongoing reference to child-raising experts. It is much worse, however, when such tutelage is imposed coercively. And, of course, lower-income people are most effectively disfranchised by the successful establishment of expert monopolies.

Professionalization is now being exacerbated by unionization of professionals. In principle, employees of nongovernment agencies can be unionized as readily as government employees. In practice, large unions prefer to deal with the large and unified management that government offers. Standards and certification become items of negotiation between union and management, thus reinforcing the drive toward professional monopolies. In addition, unions would seem to have an intrinsic antagonism toward volunteer work. It is alleged that the volunteer is an unpaid laborer and is therefore exploited. This argument has been recently advanced also by some feminists, since many volunteers are women.

In protesting the use of labor and feminist rhetoric to camouflage the establishment of coercive monopolies and the disfranchisement of people in the running of their own lives, our position is neither anti-union nor anti-feminist. Who defines exploitation? We trust people to know when they are being exploited, without the benefit of instruction by professionals, labor organizers, or feminist authors. So long as voluntary work is genuinely voluntary—is undertaken by free choice—it should be cherished and not maligned. It is of enormous value in terms of both the useful activity offered to volunteers and the actual services rendered. In addition, because of their relative freedom from bureaucratic controls, voluntary associations are important laboratories of innovation in social services; and, of course, they sustain the expression of the rich pluralism of American life.

Attacks on the volunteer principle also aid the expansion of the kind of capitalist mentality that would put a dollar sign on everything on the grounds that only that which has a price tag has worth. We believe it proper and humane (as well as "human") that there be areas of life, including public life, in which there is not a dollar sign on everything. It is debilitating to our sense of the polity to assume that only private life is to be governed by humane, nonpecuniary motives, while the rest of life is a matter of dog-eat-dog.

An additional word should be said about the development of paraprofessional fields. To be sure, people who make their living in any socially useful occupation should be given respectful recognition and should be paid a decent wage. However, much of the paraprofessional development is in fact empire-building by professional and union monopolists who would incorporate lower-status occupations into their hierarchy. At least in some instances, the word that best describes this development is exploitation. This is the case, for example, when parents and other lay people can no longer hold professionals to account because they have themselves been co-opted into the vested interests of the professionals.

With the immense growth of knowledge and skills in modern society, professions are necessary and it is inevitable that there be organizations and unions to defend their interests. This development cannot be, and should not be, reversed. It can, however, be redirected. The purpose of the professions is to serve society—not the other way around. Too often professionals regard those they serve as clients in the rather unfortunate sense the Latin word originally implied. The clients of a Roman patrician were one step above his slaves in the social hierarchy, not entirely unlike some of today's servile dependents upon professionals. Such a notion has no place in democratic society.

Professionals should be ancillary to the people they serve. Upper-income people refer to "our" doctor or "my" doctor, and whatever patterns of dependency they develop are largely of their own choosing. It should be possible for lower-income people to use the possessive pronoun in referring to professionals.

The policy implications of our approach touch also on the role of nonprofit foundations in our society. Technically, there are different kinds of foundations—strictly private, publicly supported, operating, and so on—but the current assault applies to all of them. The argument is summed up in the words of the late Wright Patman whose crusade against foundations led to Title I of the Tax Reform Act of 1969:

> Today I shall introduce a bill to end a gross inequity which this country and its citizens can no longer afford: the tax-exempt status of the so-called privately controlled charitable foundations, and their propensity for domination of business and accumulation of wealth. . . . Put most bluntly, philan-

thropy—one of mankind's more noble instincts—has been perverted into a vehicle for institutionalized deliberate evasion of fiscal and moral responsibility to the nation. (*Congressional Record*, August 6, 1969)

Of course, foundations have engaged in abuses that need to be curbed, but the resentment and hostility manifested by the curbers also needs to be curbed if we are not to harm the society very severely. The curbers of foundations make up an odd coalition. Right-wing forces are hostile to foundations because of their social experimentation (such as the Ford Foundation's programs among inner-city blacks), while others are hostile because of the role of big business ("the establishment") in funding foundations. The most dangerous part of the 1969 legislation is the new power given to the Internal Revenue Service to police foundation activities. The power to revoke or threaten to revoke tax exemption is a most effective instrument of control. (In recent years such threats have been made against religious organizations that opposed the Vietnam War and advocated sundry unpopular causes.) More ominous than the prospect that a few millionaires will get away with paying less taxes is the prospect of government control over officially disapproved advocacy or programs.

Directly related to this concern is the relatively new concept of tax expenditure that has been infiltrated into public policy. It is calculated, for example, that a certain amount of revenue is lost to the government because a private college is tax exempt. The revenue lost is called a tax expenditure. This may seem like an innocuous bit of bookkeeping, but the term expenditure implies that the college is in fact government-subsidized (a tax expenditure is a kind of government expenditure) and therefore ought to be governmentally controlled. This implication, which is made quite explicit by some bureaucrats, is incipiently totalitarian. The logic is that all of society's wealth *really* belongs to the government and that the government should therefore be able to determine how all wealth—including the wealth exempted from taxation—should be used. The concept of tax expenditure should be used, if at all, as a simple accounting device having no normative implications.

While large foundations would seem to be remote from the mediating structures under discussion, in fact they are often important to such structures at the most local level, especially in the areas of education and health. Were all these institutions taken over by the government, there might be a more uniform imposition of standards and greater financial accountability than now exists (although the monumental corruption in various government social services does not make one sanguine about the latter), but the price would be high. Massive bureaucratization, the proliferation of legal procedures that generate both public resentment and business for lawyers, the atrophying of the humane impulse, the increase of alienation—these would be some of the costs. Minimally, it should be public policy to encourage the voluntarism that, in our society, has at least slowed down these costs of modernity.

As always, the maximalist side of our approach—that is, using voluntary associations as agents of public policies—is more problematic than the minimalist. One thinks, for example, of the use of foster homes and half-way houses in the treatment and prevention of drug addiction, juvenile delinquency, and mental illness. There is reason to believe such approaches are both less costly and more effective than using bureaucratized megastructures (and their local outlets). Or one thinks of the successful resettlement of more than 100,000 Vietnam refugees in 1975, accomplished not by setting up a government agency but by working through voluntary agencies (mainly religious). This instance of using voluntary associations for public policy purposes deserves careful study. Yet another instance is the growth of the women's health movement, which in some areas is effectively challenging the monopolistic practices of the medical establishment. The ideas of people such as Ivan Illich and Victor Fuchs should be examined for their potential to empower people to reassume responsibility for their own health care. Existing experiments in decentralizing medical delivery systems should also be encouraged, with a view toward moving from decentralization to genuine empowerment.

We well know that proposals for community participation are not new. The most obvious example is the Community Action Program (CAP), a part of the War Against Poverty of the 1960s. CAP led to much disillusionment. Some condemned it as a mask for co-opting those who did, or might, threaten local power elites. Thus, community organizations were deprived of real potency and turned into government dependents. From the other side of the political spectrum, CAP was condemned for funding agitators and subversives. Yet others charged that CAP pitted community organizations against the institutions of representative government. To some extent these criticisms are mutually exclusive—they cannot all be true simultaneously. Yet no doubt all these things happened in various places in the 1960s.

That experience in no way invalidates the idea of community participation. First, the peculiar developments of the 1960s made that decade the worst possible time to try out the idea (and the same might be said about experiments in the community control of schools during the same period). Second, and much more important, the institutions used to facilitate community participation were not the actual institutions of the community but were created by those in charge of the program. This was especially true in inner-city black areas—the chief focus of the program—where religious institutions were, for the most part, neglected or even deliberately undercut. So, to some extent, were the family structures of the black community. In short, the program's failures resulted precisely from its failure to utilize existing mediating structures.

This said, it remains true that mediating structures can be co-opted by government, that they can become instruments of those interested in destroying rather than reforming American society, and that they can undermine the institutions of the formal polity. These are real risks. On the other side are the benefits described earlier. Together they constitute a major challenge to the political imagination.

VI. EMPOWERMENT THROUGH PLURALISM

The theme of pluralism has recurred many times in this essay. This final section aims simply to tie up a few loose ends, to anticipate some objections to a public policy designed to sustain pluralism through mediating structures, and to underscore some facts of *American* society that suggest both the potentials and limitations of the approach advanced here.

It should be obvious that by pluralism we mean much more than regional accents, St. Patrick's Day, and Black Pride Days, as important as all these are. Beyond providing the variety of color, costume, and custom, pluralism makes possible a tension within worlds and between worlds of meaning. Worlds of meaning put reality together in a distinctive way. Whether the participants in these worlds see themselves as mainline or subcultural, as establishment or revolutionary, they are each but part of the cultural whole. Yet the paradox is that wholeness is experienced through affirmation of the part in which one participates. This relates to the aforementioned insight of Burke regarding "the little platoon." In more contemporary psychological jargon it relates to the "identity crisis" which results from "identity diffusion" in mass society. Within one's group—whether it be racial, national, political, religious, or all of these—one discovers an answer to the elementary question, "Who am I?", and is supported in living out that answer. Psychologically and sociologically, we would propose the axiom that any identity is better than none. Politically, we would argue that it is not the business of public policy to make value judgments regarding the merits or demerits of various identity solutions, so long as all groups abide by the minimal rules that make a pluralistic society possible. It is the business of public policy not to undercut, and indeed to enhance, the identity choices available to the American people (our minimalist and maximalist propositions throughout).

This approach assumes that the process symbolized by "E Pluribus Unum" is not a zero-sum game. That is, the *unum* is not to be achieved at the expense of the *plures*. To put it positively, the national purpose indicated by the *unum* is precisely to sustain the *plures*. Of course there are tensions, and accommodations are necessary if the structures necessary to national existence are to be maintained. But in the art of pluralistic politics, such tensions are not to be eliminated but are to be welcomed as the catalysts of more imaginative accommodations. Public policy in the areas discussed in this essay has in recent decades, we believe, been too negative in its approach to the tensions of diversity and therefore too ready to impose uniform solutions on what are perceived as national social problems. In this approach, pluralism is viewed as an enemy of social policy planning rather than as a source of more diversified solutions to problems that are, after all, diversely caused and diversely defined.

Throughout this paper, we have emphasized that our proposal contains no animus toward those charged with designing and implementing social policy nor any indictment of their good intentions. The reasons for present pluralism-eroding policies are to be discovered in part in the very processes implicit in the metaphors of modernization, rationalization, and bureaucratization. The management mindset of the megastructure—whether of HEW, Sears Roebuck, or the AFL-CIO—is biased toward the unitary solution. The neat and comprehensive answer is impatient of "irrational" particularities and can only be forced to yield to greater nuance when it encounters resistance, whether from the economic market of consumer wants or from the political market of organized special interest groups. The challenge of public policy is to anticipate such resistance and, beyond that, to cast aside its adversary posture toward particularism and embrace as its goal the advancement of the multitude of particular interests that in fact constitute the common weal. Thus, far from denigrating social planning, our proposal challenges the policy maker with a much more complicated and exciting task than today's approach. Similarly, the self-esteem of the professional in all areas of social service is elevated when he or she defines the professional task in terms of being helpful and ancillary to people rather than in terms of creating a power monopoly whereby people become dependent clients.

Of course, some critics will decry our proposal as "balkanization," "retribalization," "parochialization," and such. The relevance of the Balkan areas aside, we want frankly to assert that tribe and parochial are not terms of derision. That they are commonly used in a derisive manner is the result of a worldview emerging from the late eighteenth century. That worldview held, in brief, that the laws of Nature are reflected in a political will of the people that can be determined and implemented by rational persons. Those naive notions of Nature, Will, and Reason have in the last hundred years been thoroughly discredited in almost every discipline, from psychology to sociology to physics. Yet the irony is that, although few people still believe in these myths, most social thought and planning continues to act as though they were true. The result is that the enemies of particularism ("tribalism") have become an elite tribe attempting to impose order on the seeming irrationalities of the real world and operating on premises that most Americans find both implausible and hostile to their values. Social thought has been crippled and policies have miscarried because we have not developed a paradigm of pluralism to replace the discredited assumptions of the eighteenth century. We hope this proposal is one step toward developing such a paradigm.

Throughout this essay we have frequently referred to democratic values and warned against their authoritarian and totalitarian alternatives. We are keenly aware of the limitations in any notion of "the people" actually exercising the *kratein*, the effective authority, in public policy. And we are keenly aware of how far the American polity is from demonstrating what is possible in the democratic idea. The result of political manipulation, media distortion, and the sheer weight of indifference is that the great majority of Americans have little or no political will, in the sense that term is used in democratic theory, on the great questions of domestic and international policy. Within the formal framework of democratic polity, these questions will perforce be answered by a more politicized elite. But it is precisely with respect to mediating structures that most people do have, in the most exact sense, a political will. On matters of family, church, neighborhood, hobbies, working place, and recreation, most people have a very clear idea of what is in their interest. If we are truly committed to the democratic process, it is *their* political will that public policy should be designed to empower. It may be lamentable that most Americans have no political will with respect to U.S. relations with Brazil, but that is hardly reason to undercut their very clear political will about how their children should be educated. Indeed policies that disable political will where it does exist preclude the development of political will where it does not now exist, thus further enfeebling the democratic process and opening the door to its alternatives.

As difficult as it may be for some to accept, all rational interests do not converge—or at least there is no universal agreement on what interests are rational. This means that public policy must come to terms with perduring contradictions. We need not resign ourselves to the often cynically invoked axiom that "politics is the art of the possible." In fact politics is the art of discovering *what* is possible. The possibility to be explored is not how far unitary policies can be extended before encountering the backlash of particularity. Rather, the possibility to be explored is how a common purpose can be achieved through the enhancement of myriad particular interests. This requires a new degree of modesty among those who think about social policy—not modesty in the sense of lowering our ideals in the search for meeting human needs and creating a more just society, but modesty about *our* definitions of need and justice. Every world within this society, whether it calls itself a subculture or a supraculture or simply the American culture, is in fact a subculture, is but a part of the whole. This fact needs to be systematically remembered among those who occupy the world of public policy planning and implementation.

The subculture that envisages its values as universal and its style as cosmopolitan is no less a subculture for all that. The tribal patterns evident at an Upper West Side cocktail party are no less tribal than those evident at a Polish dance in Greenpoint, Brooklyn. That the former is produced by the interaction of people trying to transcend many particularisms simply results in a new, and not necessarily more interesting, particularism. People at the cocktail party may think of themselves as liberated, and indeed they may have elected to leave behind certain particularisms into which they were born. They have, in effect, elected a new particularism. *Liberation is not escape from particularity but discovery of the particularity that fits.* Elected particularities may include life style, ideology, friendships, place of residence, and so forth. Inherited particularities may include race, economic circumstance, region, religion, and, in most cases,

43

politics. Pluralism means the lively interaction among inherited particularities and, through election, the evolution of new particularities. The goal of public policy in a pluralistic society is to sustain as many particularities as possible, in the hope that most people will accept, discover, or devise one that fits.

It might be argued that the redirection of public policy proposed here is in fact naive and quixotic. A strong argument can be made that the dynamics of modernity, operating through the megastructures and especially through the modern state, are like a great leviathan or steamroller, inexorably destroying every obstacle that gets in the way of creating mass society. There is much and ominous evidence in support of that argument. While we cannot predict the outcome of this process, we must not buckle under to alleged inevitabilities. On the more hopeful side are indications that the political will of the American people is beginning to assert itself more strongly in resistance to "massification." In contradiction of social analysts who describe the irresistible and homogenizing force of the communications media, for example, there is strong evidence that the media message is not received uncritically but is refracted through myriad world views that confound the intentions of would-be manipulators of the masses. (Happily, there are also many often-contradictory media messages.) New "Edsels" still get rejected (though the Edsel itself is a collector's item). The antiwar bias of much news about the Vietnam War (a bias we shared) was, studies suggest, often refracted in a way that reinforced support of official policy. Promotion of diverse sexual and lifestyle liberations seems to be doing little empirically verifiable damage to devotion to the family ideal. Thirty years of network TV English (not to mention thirty years of radio before that) has hardly wiped out regional dialect. In short, and to the consternation of political, cultural, and commercial purveyors of new soaps, the American people demonstrate a robust skepticism toward the modern peddlers of new worlds and a remarkable inclination to trust their own judgments. We do not wish to exaggerate these signs of hope. Counter-indicators can be listed in abundance. We do suggest there is no reason to resign ourselves to the "massification" that is so often described as America today.

America today—those words are very important to our argument. While our proposal is, we hope, relevant to modern industrialized society in general, whether socialist or capitalist, its possibilities are peculiarly attuned to the United States. (We might say, to North America, including Canada, but some aspects of particularism in Canada—for example, binationalism between French- and English-speaking Canadians—are beyond the scope of this essay.) There are at least five characteristics of American society that make it the most likely laboratory for public policy designed to enhance mediating structures and the pluralism that mediating structures make possible. First is the immigrant nature of American society. The implications of that fact for pluralism need no elaboration. Second, ours is a relatively affluent society. We have the resources to experiment toward a more humane order—for example, to place a floor of economic decency under every American. Third, this is a relatively stable society. Confronted by the prospects of neither revolution nor certain and rapid decline, we do not face the crises that call for total or definitive answers to social problems. Fourth, American society is effectively pervaded by the democratic idea and by the sense of tolerance and fair play that make the democratic process possible. This makes our society ideologically hospitable to pluralism. And fifth, however weakened they may be, we still have relatively strong institutions— political, economic, religious, and cultural—that supply countervailing forces in the shaping of social policy. Aspirations toward monopoly can, at least in theory, be challenged. And our history demonstrates that the theory has, more often than not, been acted out in practice.

Finally, we know there are those who contend that, no matter how promising all this may be for America, America is very bad for the rest of the world. It is argued that the success of America's experiment in democratic pluralism is at the expense of others, especially at the expense of the poorer nations. It is a complicated argument to which justice cannot be done here. But it might be asked, in turn, whether America would in some sense be better for the world were we to eliminate any of the five characteristics mentioned above. Were the American people more homogeneous, were they as poor as the peasants of Guatemala, were their institutions less stable and their democratic impulses less ingrained—would any of these conditions contribute concretely to a more just global order? We think not.

Neither, on the other hand, are we as convinced as some others seem to be that America is the "advance society" of human history, or at least of the modern industrialized world. Perhaps it is—perhaps not. But of *this* we are convinced: America has a singular opportunity to contest the predictions of the inevitability of mass society with its anomic individuals, alienated and impotent, excluded from the ordering of a polity that is no longer theirs. And we are convinced that mediating structures might be the agencies for a new empowerment of people in America's renewed experiment in democratic pluralism.

Cover and book design: Pat Taylor